NORTH AMERICAN INDIAN TRIBAL CHIEFS

NORTH AMERICAN
INDIAN TRIBAL
CHIEFS

KAREN LIPTAK

FRANKLIN WATTS
NEW YORK/LONDON/TORONTO/SYDNEY
A FIRST BOOK

Cover photographs copyright ©: Scala/Art Resource, N.Y./Joseph Martin (top left), The Smithsonian Institution (bottom left), The Field Museum of Natural History, Chicago (bottom right), David Koelsch (top right).

Photographs copyright ©: The Architect of the Capitol: p. 10; Art Resource, N.Y.: pp. 13 (Nefsky), 41 (Walters Gallery); The Thomas Gilcrease Institute of American History and Art, Tulsa, Oklahoma: pp. 14, 34; The Library of Congress: pp. 16, 26, 46; Nawrocki Stock Photo, Chicago: pp. 18, 38, 43; The Field Museum of Natural History, Chicago: p. 20 (#93851); The Smithsonian Institution: p. 22; North Wind Picture Archives: pp. 24, 32; The Indiana Historical Society Library: p. 27 (KCT-106); The National Museum of the American Indian, Heye Foundation: p. 29; The National Geographic Society: p. 36 (painting by Langdon Kihn); The Southwest Museum, L.A.C.A.: p. 44; The Philbrook Museum of Art, Tulsa, Oklahoma: p. 50 top; David Koelsch: p. 50 bottom; AP/Wide World Photos: pp. 51, 53; John Running Photography: p. 55; Geoff Hansen/The Valley News: p. 56.

Library of Congress Cataloging in Publication Data

Liptak, Karen.
    North American Indian tribal chiefs / Karen Liptak.
        p.   cm.—(A First book)
    Includes bibliographical references and index.
    Summary: Discusses Indian tribal chiefs in the past and present and examines the lives of four prominent chiefs, from Tecumseh to Wilma Mankiller.
    ISBN 0-531-20101-5
    1. Indians of North America—Biography—Juvenile literature.
2. Indians of North America—Politics and government—Juvenile literature.
[1. Indians of North America—Biography.   2. Indians of North America—Politics and government.]   I. Title.   II. Series.
E89.L57   1992
970.004'97022—dc20
    [B]   91-30261   CIP AC
First Paperback Edition 1992
0-531-15643-5

12/93   24427

The author extends her warm thanks to the following people for their kind help: Cherokee Principal Chief Wilma Mankiller; Winona Flying Earth and Ron McNeil, Hunkpapa Lakota (Sioux) Nation; and Martha Kreipe de Montano.

Contents

TRIBAL CHIEFS OF YESTERDAY AND TODAY

In the old days, many different North American Indian tribes lived on this continent. We use the word "chiefs" when we speak about the leaders of these tribes.

In a few tribes, chiefs had great authority over everyone. But most tribes had many leaders who answered to a council of respected elder members. Furthermore, tribes were often divided into local groups called bands, each with several chiefs. Even if the band had one main chief, that chief could command only by giving good advice that others respected.

Sometimes tribal members became temporary leaders because they had a special skill needed for a specific situation. Perhaps one could speak English at a peace talk, or another had knowledge about a new hunting ground.

But many chiefs were permanent; some gained their roles through their strong personalities and wise judgments. Others inherited their positions. Yet inheritance was not enough. Chiefs had to constantly prove themselves by everything they said and did. Otherwise, their people would stop following them.

Most chiefs were men. However, some tribes, like the Shawnee, had women chiefs. Other tribes, includ-

This painting, "The Indian Council" by Seth Eastman,
depicts a tribal meeting in which the chief is speaking
to the elders of the tribe.

ing the Cherokee, usually had male leaders, but women had the power to remove any chiefs with whom they were displeased.

Each band might have several kinds of chiefs, but the main ones were the war chiefs and peace chiefs. The peace chiefs were wise, caring, and spiritual people who could speak for the group "in council" (at talks) with other bands, other tribes, and non-Indians. They also handled the daily affairs of their people.

War chiefs were outstanding warriors who could lead war and raiding parties to victory. In some tribes, peace chiefs were forbidden to serve as war chiefs. Elsewhere, the events of their day led peacemakers to arm themselves and become war chiefs, too.

A band might also have subchiefs and religious leaders. Subchiefs led family groups. Religious leaders performed ceremonies and rituals. Leaders would yield to those best able to handle situations as they came up. Some conditions required the chief of one band to become the principal chief over many bands. But when the condition ended, the chief returned to heading one band.

Welcome Turns to Warfare

When tribal leaders first met Europeans in the 1500s, many welcomed the newcomers from across the sea.

After all, Mother Earth had plenty of land for everyone. Besides, the white-skinned people brought desirable items that the Indians got from them in trade. These included metal tools and weapons, cloth, and spices.

But the welcome did not last very long. The early explorers were followed by fur trappers, miners, settlers, and others. Some unknowingly carried diseases, such as smallpox, measles, and influenza, from which many Native Americans died. Just as deadly to the Indians was the attitude many Europeans held about the Indian homelands. The newcomers wanted the land for themselves!

After the United States became a nation in 1783, settlers poured into the new country. Blinded by the freedoms they had gained, these new Americans failed to see that they were taking freedoms away from the First Americans. They pushed westward, moving onto Indian lands. Meanwhile, the federal government wanted to build roads and railroad tracks through Indian country in order to connect the United States from east coast to west coast.

While some government officials sympathized with the Indians' claims to the land, federal policy was to support United States citizens and national interests. Federal authorities began using promises or threats to make tribal chiefs sign "peace treaties."

The treaties promised benefits to tribes who gave

"The Approach of the Wagon Train," a painting
by William Cary, shows an Indian warrior
watching the advance of white settlers.

Indian tribes were forced to defend
their lands in this painting
by Frederic Remington.

up their homelands and moved onto "reservations"—tracts of land that were usually much smaller than the tribes' original territories. The benefits promised included schools, shops, yearly payments, clothes, and government protection. Tribes or bands who refused the offers faced the mighty United States Army.

Many chiefs signed the treaties—some with hope, others in despair. Sometimes United States officials appointed "chiefs." These were often cooperative tribal members who signed away their bands' homelands. Other Indians called these appointees "government chiefs."

But many tribal leaders rose to defend their people and their land. Some gave eloquent speeches that we still quote today. Others won fame as valiant warriors. But all of them faced an enemy who would not honor their rights as people, nor respect their spiritual bond to Mother Earth.

A Continuing Struggle

The struggle for Indian rights and respect continues today, although modern tribal leaders usually defend their peoples' interests in a new battlefield—the courtroom. Another change is that women now play larger roles in Native American politics; about 40 of the 504 tribes in the United States are now led by women.

In this lithograph by J. O. Lewis, the Treaty of Prairie du Chien was signed by representatives of Indian tribes and government officials. The treaty defined the boundaries of land claims in the old Northwest.

Today, as in the past, there are many outstanding tribal leaders. Choosing just four for this book wasn't easy, but those selected are meant to provide a view of different tribes, historical periods, and leadership styles.

You will meet three great historical leaders: Tecumseh of the Shawnee, Young Joseph of the Nez Percé, and Sitting Bull of the Sioux. A fourth leader presented here is Wilma Mankiller, today's elected principal chief of the Cherokee of Oklahoma. Her concerns will help you understand some of the problems that North American Indians now face.

As you read, remember that our Native American "history" largely comes from reports by Europeans, since in the past most Indians in the United States had no written language. Because outsiders wrote these reports, the account of what happened is sometimes distorted. Then, too, some tribes forbade the keeping of family histories. For instance, until recent times, the Apache would not say a person's name after death, so as not to anger the spirit of the dead.

Remember, too, that although many tribal leaders gained national fame for their skill in battles and their stirring speeches, Native Americans consider their greatest chiefs primarily spiritual people. Respected leaders were devoted to their people, to their land,

An Indian historian uses painting
to pass on the tribe's history to
a younger member of the tribe.

and to the Great Spirit. North American Indians of today still seek these qualities in those they choose as leaders.

"Sell a country! Why not sell the air, the great sea as well as the earth? Did not the Great Spirit make them all for the use of his children?"

TECUMSEH
(*ca.* 1768–1813) *Shawnee*

Tecumseh was a man with a great dream: to bring together all North American tribes into one Indian nation. He was born in a village on the Mad River near what is today Springfield, Ohio. He was the son of a Shawnee war leader and a woman who was possibly of mixed Creek and Cherokee ancestry. Tecumseh's name means "Shooting Star." He is said to have had a great sense of his own destiny. As a child, he seemed to know that he would someday do great things for his people.

When Tecumseh was young, during the Revolutionary War period, the Shawnee were a nomadic peo-

In this portrait of Tecumseh,
the chief is dressed in
western clothing.

ple, living in groups scattered through the Ohio region. After the war ended in 1783, American settlers started flocking westward, toward the area that the Shawnee and their allies called home.

Before Tecumseh was seven, his father was killed in a battle against Americans. Tecumseh's training in survival skills was taken over by his older brother, Cheeseekau. At age nineteen, he and Cheeseekau went south to join the Cherokee in their fight against white settlers moving into the region.

Cheeseekau was killed in that campaign, but Tecumseh spent three years as leader of a Shawnee band allied to the Cherokee. Tecumseh returned to his homeland around 1790.

In 1795, he faced non-Indians once again. United States officials were urging the Shawnee and other tribes to sell huge land parcels as part of the Fort Greenville Treaty. Tecumseh believed that the land belonged to all Indians; therefore, no single Indian or tribe had the right to sell land to non-Indians. And, since the land was owned by all Indians, every tribe had to help defend it against invaders.

Along with many followers who also opposed the treaty, Tecumseh moved to what is now Indiana. There, a non-Indian schoolteacher, Rebecca Galloway, helped him to learn English and study world history and literature. His education helped Tecumseh to develop

Another portrait of Tecumseh shows him in a combination of western and Indian clothing.

an effective speaking style that he used in his crusade for a unified Indian nation.

Tecumseh was helped by his brother, a medicine man and prophet who called himself Tenskwatawa (Open Door). Tenskwatawa was known by non-Indians as the Shawnee Prophet. He claimed an ability to see things that were to come.

One day, upon reviving from a trance, Tenskwa-tawa announced that he had visited the Spirit World and been told that someday he would be able to make dead animals and spirits rise, along with dead warriors and friends of the Indians. He preached a return to traditional Indian ways and denounced the non-Indians' customs, clothes, and use of alcohol.

Tecumseh and Tenskwatawa set up a village known as Prophetstown on the bank of the Tippecanoe River in what is now Indiana. Soon, the two brothers were a powerful team. Tenskwatawa urged religious revival, while Tecumseh toured the Middle West and South, calling for a league of Indian groups.

In 1809, William Henry Harrison, then governor of the Indiana Territory, convinced some Shawnee chiefs to accept a meager amount of money for three million acres of Indian land. Tecumseh was outraged when he heard about this.

The next year, with a huge group of warriors from many tribes, Tecumseh met with Harrison at Vincennes, in today's Indiana. Once more, Tecumseh protested that land sales were not valid unless every Indian agreed to them, saying, "A single twig breaks, but the bundle of twigs is strong. Someday I will embrace our brother tribes and draw them into a bundle and together we will win our country back from the whites."

Harrison was impressed with Tecumseh, referring

The Indian prophet Tenskwatawa relates
his visions to other members
of his tribe.

to him later as an "uncommon genius." But the two
reached no agreement.

    After the Vincennes Council ended, Tecumseh was
more eager than ever to unite all Indians from Canada
to the Gulf of Mexico. Harrison feared the effect of

Tecumseh's powerful speeches. He wanted to stop the Indian movement before it was too late.

On November 7, 1811, while Tecumseh was in the South trying to gain more support for his alliance, Harrison marched with nine hundred soldiers against Prophetstown on the Tippecanoe. Tenskwatawa, who had been left in charge of the village, was lured into a battle for which his people were unprepared. Many Shawnee fled, enabling Harrison's troops to enter and destroy the town. While the Battle of Tippecanoe was not a major victory for the army, it destroyed the faith Tenskwatawa's followers had in him and weakened Tecumseh's movement.

Soon afterward, the War of 1812 broke out between the British and the Americans. Tecumseh's struggle for Indian unity was hurt even more. Along with many other Indians, he joined the British army, hoping to help defeat the Americans.

The British made Tecumseh a brigadier general, and the great statesman now devoted himself to leading his Indian troops in many campaigns. On October 5, 1813, at the Thames River in southern Ontario, Canada, Harrison's troops completely defeated the combined British and Indian forces. Tecumseh was killed in the battle. Some report that he foresaw his end, and therefore went to that day's battle in Indian dress rather than in that of the British army.

At the age of forty-five, Tecumseh died, taking with

William Henry Harrison, at the Battle of Tippecanoe. The predawn attack had taken his camp by surprise.

The Battle of the Thames
resulted in the death
of Tecumseh.

him the dream of an Indian nation in North America. Without his tireless campaigning, an Indian alliance on the grand scale he dreamed of was never formed.

"The earth is the mother of all people, and all people should have equal rights upon it."

CHIEF JOSEPH
(ca. 1840–1904) Nez Percé

Young Joseph was one of five children born in the Wallowa Valley of northeastern Oregon to a respected chief known as Old Joseph and a Nez Percé mother. While his brother Ollokot was considered a daring fighter, Young Joseph was regarded as a thinker by his people. Yet this man who spoke so thoughtfully in council was to become a great military commander.

During Joseph's childhood, the Nez Percé were friendly with the Europeans, whom they first met when French fur trappers reached the Northwest in the mid-1700s. As Joseph grew up, more and more Europeans began living in the fertile Wallowa Valley. The Walla Walla Treaty of 1855 reduced the tribe's land, allowing additional settlers to move into the region. When gold

Chief Joseph, in traditional
Indian costume

was discovered in the early 1860s, still more non-Indians rushed there.

In 1863, United States federal officials convinced several Nez Percé chiefs to sell most of the tribe's remaining land. The new treaty they agreed to called for the people to settle on the Lapwai Reservation in what is today Idaho. But Old Joseph and many other chiefs ignored the treaty. They stayed in their beloved Wallowa Valley, outside the new reservation.

When Young Joseph was thirty-one, in 1871, he replaced his ailing father as a leader. Four years later the government—under pressure from settlers and prospectors—agreed to open the Wallowa Valley to white homesteaders.

As a result, the longtime peace between the Nez Percé and non-Indians came to an end. Although Joseph tried to keep his people calm, the settlers feared a possible attack. They demanded military protection.

In May 1877, General Oliver O. Howard was sent into the Wallowa Valley. Howard often supported Indian rights, but he was also a dedicated army officer. He told Joseph and the other chiefs who had not agreed to the 1863 treaty that they had to relocate to the Lapwai Reservation in one month. Otherwise, he would use force to bring them in.

Joseph knew that the army greatly outnumbered his men. The younger braves urged him to resist, but

Joseph directed his band to gather their belongings and head north to Lapwai. However, while his people rested at Rocky Canyon, three young Nez Percé warriors returned south, seeking revenge. Other Indians joined them to raid the settlements and kill settlers.

When Joseph heard what had happened, he knew that war would come. To protect his people, he led them south, to the bottom of White Bird Canyon. There, on June 17, 1877, United States soldiers rode into the camp, where six Indians with a truce flag were waiting. When soldiers fired at them, concealed warriors shot back. The Nez Percé War was on.

Not wanting his people to surrender or to be killed, Chief Joseph chose retreat as their best option. He led eight hundred women, men, and children on a flight across the Bitterroot Mountains to join their allies, the Crow Indians, in Montana. Pursued by General Howard and his troops, Joseph guided the Nez Percé along twisting mountain trails, across deep rivers, and over long stretches of barren plains. They fought at least thirteen battles, yet treated all the settlers they met in the Bitterroot Valley with respect.

But when the Nez Percé reached Montana, they were denied help by the Crow, who feared the army's strength. A new plan was agreed upon: to head north and flee across the border to safety in Canada.

The Nez Percé continued on, in one of the most

Twisting mountain trails made
it difficult for the army to
follow the Nez Percé.

courageous military retreats in this country's history. Finally, the exhausted fugitives reached the Bear Paw Mountains, Montana. They were less than thirty miles from Canada when Colonel Nelson Miles and his men staged a surprise dawn attack on September 30, 1877. As a blizzard began, Joseph's starving band used cooking utensils and their shivering hands to build trenches and dugouts.

The five-day Battle of Bear Paws that followed resulted in heavy losses on both sides. Joseph knew that escape was possible, if the Nez Percé left behind their wounded, and their old women and children. But that was not his way. On October 5, a day after General Howard caught up with Colonel Miles's troops, a weary Chief Joseph met with the two officers to talk peace.

His words of surrender were filled with a sadness that can be felt through all ages. Chief Joseph told of great Nez Percé leaders, including Looking Glass and Toohoolhoolzote, who had died in the battle. (Joseph's brother, Ollokot, had also been killed.) Joseph told of his people starving and freezing to death. He told of his own children missing. "Hear me, my chiefs! I am tired," he said. "My heart is sick and sad. From where the sun now stands, I will fight no more forever."

Colonel Miles promised that the Nez Percé could return to the Northwest, and settle on the Lapwai Res-

Chief Joseph's surrender to Colonel Nelson Miles on October 4, 1877

ervation. But against his protests, the federal government sent the Nez Percé to Indian Territory in what is now Oklahoma and Kansas. There, in an unfamiliar land, many of Joseph's people became sick and died.

Twice, Joseph visited Washington to plead for his people. "Treat all men alike," he urged officials. "Give them all the same law. Give them all an even chance to live and grow. All men were made by the Great Spirit Chief. They are all brothers."

Joseph's heartfelt words touched people across the United States, and many appealed to the government to help his cause. Finally, in 1885, the Nez Percé were allowed to return to the Northwest. Some were relocated to Lapwai. Others, like Joseph, were assigned to the Colville Reservation in Washington State. There, the government offered Joseph a modern house, but he chose to remain in a traditional tepee.

On September 21, 1904, after outliving all of his nine children, sixty-four-year-old Joseph suddenly fell over and died while sitting before his fire. According to the reservation doctor, his death was caused by "a broken heart."

In June 1905, a white marble monument was erected at Nespelem, Washington, in memory of Chief Joseph. Inscribed on it is his tribal name, "Hinmaton Yalatkit," and its English translation, "Thunder-rolling in the mountains."

Chief Joseph, the "greatest of Indian strategists"

Chief Yellow Bull spoke at the dedication ceremony, "Joseph is dead, but his words ... will live forever." Today, people of all races continue to quote Chief Joseph and to hope, as he did, that, "no more groans of wounded men and women will ever go to the ear of the Great Spirit Chief above, and that all people may be one people."

"If the Great Spirit desired me to be a white man He would have made me so in the first place.... Each man is good in His sight. It is not necessary for eagles to be crows."

SITTING BULL
(1831–1890) *Hunkpapa Sioux*

As a boy living near the Grand River in what is now South Dakota, Sitting Bull had a number of childhood names. One of these was Hunka Sni, which means slow, because, as Sitting Bull's great-great-great-grandson, Ron McNeil explains, "He did things deliberately ... never impatiently."

The Sioux chief Sitting Bull

At age fourteen, after proving himself a brave warrior in a raid against the Crow—longtime enemies of the Sioux—Hunka Sni's proud father gave him a new name. It was one that he had received in a vision: Tatanka Yotanka, or Sitting Bull.

Like his father, Sitting Bull had visions that told him about the future. He was also a religious man who prayed to the Creator in times of need. While still a youth, he was accepted into the Strong Hearts, an elite warriors' society. However, Sitting Bull was respected for much more than his military skill. As Hunkpapa Indian Winona Flying Earth recently explained, "He had spiritual qualities that the people admired. Therefore, his opinions were highly regarded."

In 1860, when Sitting Bull became a leader of the Hunkpapa Sioux, non-Indians were invading Sioux territory from both the east and the west. In retaliation, Chief Red Cloud of the Oglala Sioux led vigorous attacks against trespassers along the Bozeman Trail, a direct route through Sioux land to the gold fields in what is now Montana. Other Sioux bands also attacked the settlers and soldiers around them. By 1868, the United States government was eager to meet with Sioux leaders and make peace.

The Treaty of Fort Laramie resulted from these talks. It stated that the federal government would stop using the Bozeman Trail, and would give the Sioux and their allies a huge reservation in what is now western South Dakota. The government also pledged that the Indians could hunt buffalo forever in the Powder River Country, near the reservation. This area would remain closed to non-Indians.

Red Cloud and many other Sioux leaders signed the new treaty, but Sitting Bull did not. He had refused to attend the peace talks, saying, "I will not have my people robbed." Along with other Hunkpapa who had not signed the treaty, he continued to live off the reservation, in the Powder River Country.

But non-Indians kept intruding on Sioux land. Their numbers rose sharply after 1874, when gold was reported in the Black Hills of South Dakota. The Black Hills, which are sacred to the Sioux, had been guaranteed to them by the Fort Laramie Treaty. Despite the treaty, hundreds of miners rushed there when news of the gold spread.

Since the miners would not leave, the United States government urged the Sioux to sell the land. After the Sioux refused, the government ordered all hunting bands to report at once to the reservation. When Sitting Bull and the other non-treaty leaders refused, army troops went after them.

Sitting Bull set up camp with the Sioux and their allies, the Cheyenne and Arapaho, at Rosebud Creek in what is now southern Montana. The camp quickly

The Sioux set up camp outside
Fort Laramie in preparation
for the Treaty of Laramie.

grew. By June 1876, it was three miles long and was filled with warriors preparing for battle. Meanwhile, the army moved in for a showdown.

Which side would win? Sitting Bull sought a guiding vision from the Great Spirit through performing the Sun Dance, a traditional ceremony of the Plains. He sacrificed pieces of his flesh so that his prayers might be answered. Then he danced for over a day, without food or drink. Finally, he slumped to the ground, unconscious. He saw a vision of dead soldiers falling from the sky into his camp. Upon reviving, he interpreted his vision: the Sioux would be victorious.

On June 17, warriors led by Crazy Horse drove away army troops under General George Crook at Rosebud. But it was not a clear victory. Sitting Bull's vision was yet to come true.

On June 25, Lieutenant Colonel George Armstrong Custer and his Seventh Cavalry began a surprise attack on the Indian camp on Montana's Little Bighorn River. But Custer had blundered by commanding his men to fight without waiting for reinforcements. Furthermore, he divided his forces, even though he knew they were greatly outnumbered.

The Indian warriors charged back at the attacking army troops, and wiped out at least 250 men, including Custer and his entire cavalry. It was the United States

The Battle of Little Bighorn,
June 25, 1876

Long after Little Bighorn,
Kicking Bear, a veteran of the battle,
painted his version of the fighting.

Army's worst defeat in its battles with the North American Indians.

The army continued the military campaign against the Indians. Many leaders surrendered, but Sitting Bull fled to Canada with his people. He warned them not to believe the Americans, who "take from the poor and weak to support the rich who rule." Yet, many of his people, weakened by harsh conditions in Canada, returned to the reservation. Many others died from lack of food and the cold.

Finally, in July 1881, Sitting Bull and his few remaining warriors surrendered. Afterward, he was confined at Fort Randall, South Dakota, for two years, then sent to the Standing Rock Reservation in that same state. By then he was world famous as the Indian leader who had defeated General Custer.

In 1885 Sitting Bull toured the eastern states with a wild west show directed by Buffalo Bill Cody, who became his good friend. Some Hunkpapa Indians think that he went on tour in order to tell non-Indians about his people. Others believe that he left the reservation because government officials were after him. However, he refused a second tour, and returned home, where his people were being pressured to sell more land. Sitting Bull cautioned them not to give away more of their heritage. Other Sioux leaders argued that if they refused, their land would be taken away from them anyway. Eventually, the Sioux were forced to sell 11 million acres, and the government broke up their reservation into several smaller ones.

Sitting Bull once used to sing all the time as he walked around the camp. One of his favorite songs was "Be cheerful now. Have a holiday spirit. Do not have

Chief Sitting Bull,
in traditional dress,
with Buffalo Bill Cody

special friends. Be friends with everyone." But he must have found it harder and harder to sing, for there were disturbing changes everywhere.

The government banned traditional ceremonies and rituals—including the Sun Dance, one of the sacred rites the Sioux had received from the Great Spirit. The government also set up a police force, composed of Indians, to enforce federal rules. Generations-old hunting parties were now replaced by government food rations. Poor crops and epidemics added to the Sioux misery. As despair spread, many turned to a new religion for hope.

Called the Ghost Dance Religion by non-Indians, the new faith was founded by a young Paiute Indian mystic named Wovoka. He preached that a brighter future awaited those Indians who renounced non-Indian ways and returned to the old life-style.

Although Sitting Bull did not totally embrace Wovoka's faith, he didn't stop others from following it. Reservation officials were less tolerant. They feared that the Ghost Dance Religion would lead to rebellion led by Sitting Bull. "You should say nothing against our religion for we say nothing against yours … we both pray to only one God who made us all," he argued. Nevertheless, the old leader's arrest was ordered.

Early on December 15, 1890, forty-three Indian policemen came to Sitting Bull's cabin to take him away. At first he went willingly. But after being hustled outside, and seeing many followers watching him, he shouted out, "I'm not going."

The fight that followed took the lives of six policemen and eight of Sitting Bull's followers, including his seventeen-year-old son, Crowfoot. Sitting Bull, too, was killed, from guns fired by tribal policemen.

Years after Sitting Bull's death, one of his descendants dreamed of the Sun Dance being performed in front of Sitting Bull's home, in the beautiful valley close to the Grand River. Today, the Sun Dance is held there annually.

Meanwhile, Sitting Bull remains a hero to the Hunkpapa. As Winona Flying Earth explains, "He didn't consider himself out of the ordinary.... He was a leader of the people, but he also completely respected all the people." At Standing Rock College on the reservation, this quote from Sitting Bull appears on all stationery: "Let's put our minds together to see what we can build for the future."

"People should have a great pride in their history and heritage and use that as a source of strength in making decisions."

WILMA MANKILLER
(born 1945) Cherokee

Cherokee culture thrived for hundreds of years in the southeastern United States. Then, in 1838, some 18,000 Cherokee were forced by the United States government on a 1,200-mile-long march to relocate in Oklahoma. Thousands of Cherokee died on the journey, which came to be known as "The Trail of Tears." Among those who survived were the ancestors of Wilma Mankiller. (Mankiller is a common Cherokee family name.) The surviving Cherokee regrouped in Oklahoma and set up an Indian nation that is today the second largest in the country.

Wilma Mankiller, who would grow up to become the first female chief of the Cherokee, was born to a Dutch-Irish mother and a Cherokee father in Tahlequah, Oklahoma. As one of eleven children, she spent her early years on Mankiller Flats, land her grandfather had received from the United States government.

At age twelve, after severe droughts ruined the family farm, Mankiller's family moved to San Francisco, California. They entered a federal program that found work in the cities for rural Indians. In the city, Mankiller's father became a warehouse worker and a union organizer. During the 1960s, Wilma Mankiller studied at San Francisco State University.

In 1969, she watched young Indians take over a former prison to protest the poor treatment of Indians. Since she was married and had two young daughters, Mankiller didn't feel she could be an active protester.

"The Endless Trail,"
a painting by Jerome Tiger,
illustrates the tragedy
of the 1,200-mile march
by the Cherokee.

Chief Wilma Mankiller,
leader of the Cherokee

Indians on Alcatraz, getting their
water in glass jugs brought to
the island by boat

However, she raised funds for the activists, and her desire to help her people grew.

In 1976, after her marriage ended, Mankiller took her daughters back to Oklahoma, and built a small house on her grandfather's land. She earned a bachelor of arts degree and started working on economic projects for the Cherokee Nation.

Then, a car accident in 1979 forced her to spend a year at home, recuperating. While regaining her strength, she thought about what the Cherokee elders call "being of good mind." This involves thinking positively, accepting everyone as family, and using the past to improve the future. She believes that what she learned during this period has helped her become a better leader.

In 1981, as founder and first director of the Cherokee Nation's Community Development Department, she began several community self-help programs. These included housing and educational reforms and were well received. She was respected too for her compassion and vision.

The principal chief, Ross Swimmer, ran for reelection in 1983, and chose Mankiller as his running mate. Their election made her the first female deputy principal chief in Cherokee history. Two years later, after Swimmer resigned to head the Bureau of Indian Affairs,

Chief Wilma Mankiller and Chief Phillip Martin
of the Mississippi band of Choctaw Indians
testify before a Senate Indian Affairs
Special Investigations subcommittee.

Mankiller became principal chief of the Cherokee of Oklahoma. It was another first for a Cherokee woman.

Women play a strong role in Cherokee society. In the old days, they trained male leaders and held a women's council. But then the people became used to male chiefs. This made Chief Mankiller's new job difficult at first. However, when she ran for reelection in 1987, she was voted into office again.

Chief Mankiller governs 105,000 Cherokee. She has managed social programs and business ventures that are improving the rights and economic conditions of the Cherokee Nation. Her work has been aimed at lowering her people's high unemployment rate, and raising their level of education and health care.

Another of Mankiller's aims has been for the Cherokee to be self-reliant. "We need to trust our own thinking," she has said, "and not think that some expert somewhere has better ideas about how we should live and what our future communities should look like." She has striven to combine the most valuable parts of the modern non-Indian world with the best of the old ways of life.

Mankiller also has tried to educate non-Indians about Native Americans. In a recent speech she noted, "People still think we live in tepees and wear tribal garb every day. But we wear business suits and dresses and drive station wagons—not horses."

One of the old ways of life
that Chief Mankiller has tried to
preserve is illustrated in this
traditional Cherokee powwow.

Chief Wilma Mankiller, receiving
an Honorary Doctorate from
Dartmouth College in June 1991

Wilma Mankiller's work has won her many awards and honors. Among these have been Woman of the Year from *Ms.* magazine (1987), American Indian Woman of the Year from the Oklahoma Federation of Indian Women (1986), and an Honorary Doctorate from Yale University.

Mankiller has remarried and has become a grand-mother. She works with other female Indian leaders, including Mildred Cleghorn, the first female chairperson of the Chiricahua Apache.

Mankiller was reelected for a third term in June 1991. She has become a model for young Cherokee girls. Before her election, they "would never have thought they might grow up to be chief," she recently observed. "Now they realize they can achieve anything they want."

GLOSSARY

Band—A division of a tribe.

Black Hills—Sacred land for the Sioux Indians located in what is now South Dakota.

Cavalry—A unit of soldiers on horseback.

Cherokee—A North American Indian tribe. Today most Cherokee live in Oklahoma, where they were forcibly relocated from the Southeast in 1838. They are known as the Cherokee of Oklahoma. Some Cherokee escaped removal and now have a reservation at Cherokee, North Carolina. They are known as the Eastern Band of Cherokee.

Cheyenne—North American Indian tribe originally living around Lake Superior, then moving to the Great Plains.

Great Spirit—The highest spiritual force to North American Indians.

Hunkpapa—A division of the Sioux (also known as the Teton Dakota or Western Sioux), to which Chief Sitting Bull belonged.

Nez Percé—North American Indian tribe located in western Idaho, northeastern Oregon, and southwestern Washington.

Paiute—North American Indian tribe of the West, today primarily in Arizona, California, Nevada, Oregon, and Utah.

Powder River Country—Former buffalo hunting grounds of the Sioux in what is now South Dakota.

Reservation—A tract of land held in trust by the federal government for North American Indians and managed by the Bureau of Indian Affairs.

Reservation Agent—An official appointed by the United States government to be in charge of a reservation.

Revolutionary War—The War for Independence that began on April 19, 1775, and ended with a final treaty signed on September 3, 1783.

Shawnee—North American Indians who moved from the Ottawa Valley of Ontario and Quebec to the Ohio Valley.

Sioux—North American Indians who were originally woodlands people and became nomadic buffalo hunters of the Plains.

Wallowa Valley—Northeastern Oregon home of the Nez Percé.

FOR FURTHER READING

Bealer, Alex W. *Only the Names Remain: The Cherokees and the Trail of Tears*. Boston: Little Brown, 1972.

Halliburton, Warren. *The Tragedy of Little Bighorn*. New York: Franklin Watts, 1989.

Highwater, Jamake. *Many Smokes, Many Moons: A Chronology of American Indian History Through Indian Art*. Philadelphia: Lippincott, 1978.

Hook, Jason. *Sitting Bull and the Plains Indians*. New York: The Bookwright Press, 1987.

Landau, Elaine. *The Sioux*. New York: Franklin Watts, 1989.

May, Robin. *North American Indians*. Englewood Cliffs, NJ: Silver Burdett, 1978.

Montgomery, Elizabeth Rider. *Chief Joseph, Guardian of His People*. Champaign, IL: Garrard Publishing Co., 1969.

Stevenson, Augusta. *Tecumseh, Shawnee Boy*. Indianapolis: Bobbs-Merrill, 1962.

Watson, Jane Werner. *The First Americans*. New York: Pantheon Books, 1980.

For More Advanced Readers

Freedman, Russell. *Indian Chiefs*. New York: Holiday House, 1987.

INDEX

Harrison, William Henry 23–26
Howard, Oliver, 30, 31, 33
Hunkpapa Sioux, 37–48, 58
Hunting, 40, 47, 59

Indian Nation, 19, 22, 25, 28, 49
Indian Territory, 35

Joseph, Chief, 17, 28–37

Kicking Bear, 44

Land rights, 12, 14, 15, 16, 21, 23, 30, 40, 45
Lapwai Reservation, 30, 31, 33, 35
Little Bighorn, 42, 43, 44

Mankiller, Wilma, 17, 48–57
Martin, Phillip, 53
Miles, Nelson, 33, 34
Montana, 31, 33, 39, 40, 42

Nez Percé, 17, 28–37, 58, 59

Oklahoma, 17, 35, 49, 52, 54, 58
Old Joseph, 28, 30
Ollokot, 28, 33

Paiute Indians, 47, 58
Powder River Country, 40, 59
Prophetstown, 23, 25

Red Cloud, 39, 40
Religion, 11, 23, 39, 47
Reservation Agent, 59
Reservations, 15, 30, 35, 40, 45, 47, 48, 58, 59
Retreat, 31, 33
Revolutionary War, 19, 21, 59

Settlers, white 11, 12, 13, 17, 21, 28, 30, 31, 39
Shawnee, 9, 17, 19–28, 23, 25, 59
Shawnee Prophet, 22
Sioux, 17, 37–48, 58, 59